the glucose revolution

top 100 G.I. foods

ASSOC. PROFESSOR JENNIE BRAND-MILLER • KAYE FOSTER-POWELL
DR ANTHONY LEEDS

coronet

Copyright © 1998 by Assoc. Professor Jennie Brand-Miller, Kaye Foster-Powell and Dr Anthony Leeds

The right of Assoc. Professor Jennie Brand-Miller, Kaye Foster-Powell and Dr Anthony Leeds to be identified as the Author of the Work has been asserted by them in accordance with the Copyright, Designs and Patents Act 1988.

First published in Australia in 1998 by
Hodder Headline Australia Pty Limited

First published in Great Britain in 2002 by Hodder and Stoughton
A division of Hodder Headline

This United Kingdom edition is published by arrangement with
Hodder Headline Australia Pty Limited
A Coronet paperback

10 9 8 7 6 5 4 3

A CIP catalogue record for this title is available from the British Library

0 340 77056 2

Typeset in Minion and Gill Sans by
Phoenix Typesetting, Ilkley, West Yorkshire

Printed in Great Britain by Clays Ltd, St Ives plc

Hodder and Stoughton
A division of Hodder Headline
338 Euston Road
London NW1 3BH

CONTENTS

All-Bran™ • Apples • Apple juice • Apricots • Baked Beans • Bananas • Barley • Basmati rice • Black-eyed beans • Bran Buds™ • Bread • Bread Mixed Grain • Buckwheat • Bulgur • Bush foods • Butter beans • Cereal grains • Chapati-baisen • Cherries • Chick peas • Chocolate • Custard • Dairy foods • Digestive biscuits • Dried apricots • Fettuccine • Frosties™ • Fructose • Fruit • Fruit cocktail • Fruit loaf • Grapefruit • Grapes • Highland oatmeal biscuits • Honey • Ice cream • Instant noodles • Kidney beans • Kiwi fruit • Lactose • Legumes • Lentils • Lima beans • Lungkow bean thread noodles • M&Ms™ • Macaroni • Mangoes • Milk • Muesli • Mung beans • Navy/haricot beans • New potatoes, canned • Nutella™ • Oat bran • Oranges • Orange juice • Pasta • Pawpaw • Peanuts • Peaches • Pears • Peas, green •

Peas, dried • Pineapple juice • Pinto beans • Pitta bread • Ploughman's Wholegrain Loaf • Plums • Popcorn • Porridge • Potato crisps • Pumpernickel • Quick cooking wheat • Ravioli • Red kidney beans • Rice bran • Rich tea biscuits • Semolina • Skimmed milk • So Good™ • Sourdough Rye bread • Soy & Linseed Loaf • Soy beans • Spaghetti • Special K™ • Split peas • Sponge cake • Sultana Bran™ • Sultanas • Sweet corn • Sweet potato • Tomato soup • Tortellini • Vegetables • Vermicelli • Whole wheat kernels • Whole kernel rye • Yam • Yoghurt

WHAT THE G.I. FACTOR IS ALL ABOUT

Worldwide research since the early 1980s has shown us that different carbohydrate foods have dramatically different effects on blood sugar levels. Until very recently it was widely believed that complex carbohydrates, such as rice and potato were best for us. They were thought to be slowly digested energy foods that caused only a small rise in our blood sugar levels. Sugars on the other hand, have been seen as villains that cause rapid fluctuations in blood sugar levels. The G.I. research has turned all these beliefs upside down and changed the way we think about carbohydrates.

When scientists began to study the actual blood sugar responses to different foods in hundreds of people, they found that many starchy foods (bread, potatoes) are digested and absorbed very quickly and that many sugar-containing foods were actually quite slowly absorbed.

The glycaemic index (or G.I. factor as we have called it) was developed simply as a means of ranking foods based on their immediate effect on our blood sugar levels. Carbohydrate foods that break down quickly during digestion have the highest G.I. factors. The blood sugar response is fast and high. In other words the glucose (or sugar) in the bloodstream increases rapidly. Conversely, carbohydrates which break down slowly, releasing glucose gradually into the bloodstream have low G.I. factors.

The substance which produces the greatest rise in blood sugar levels is pure glucose itself. All other foods have less effect when fed in equal amounts of carbohydrate. The G.I. factor of pure glucose is set at 100 and every other food is ranked on a scale from 0 to 100 according to its actual effect on blood sugar levels.

Today we know the G.I. factors of hundreds of different food items that have been tested following the standardised method. The complete table of the G.I. factors of hundreds of foods can be found in our original book, *The Glucose Revolution* (Hodder & Stoughton, 2000).

HOW CAN YOU BENEFIT FROM LOW G.I. FOODS?

The slow digestion and gradual rise and fall in blood sugar levels after a low G.I. food has benefits for many people. Foremost, it helps control blood sugar levels in people with diabetes. It also reduces the secretion of the hormone insulin into the blood, high levels being undesirable because they increase the risk of heart disease, diabetes and obesity. Thus low G.I. foods are of benefit to people with and without diabetes.

Low G.I. foods:
- result in lower insulin levels which makes fat easier to burn and less likely to be stored
- help to lower blood fats
- are more satisfying and reduce appetite
- help to sustain endurance exercise for longer
- reduce our risk of developing diabetes
- reduce our risk of developing heart disease

These facts are not an exaggeration. They are confirmed results of studies published in prestigious journals by scientists around the world.

SOURCES OF CARBOHYDRATE

Carbohydrate mainly comes from plant foods, such as cereal grains, fruits, vegetables and legumes (peas and beans). Milk products also contain carbohydrate. Some foods contain a large amount of carbohydrate (e.g. cereals, potatoes, legumes) while other foods are very dilute sources e.g. carrots, broccoli, salad vegetables. The dilute sources can be eaten freely, but they won't provide anywhere near enough carbohydrate for our high-carbohydrate diet. A salad is not a meal and must be completed by a carbohydrate-dense food such as bread. The following list includes foods that are high in carbohydrate and provide very little fat. Eat lots of them, sparing the butter, margarine and oil during their preparation.

Cereal grains including rice, wheat, oats, barley, rye and anything made from them (bread, pasta, breakfast cereal, flour).

Fruits such as apples, oranges, bananas, grapes, peaches, melons etc.

Vegetables such as potatoes, yams, sweet corn, and sweet potato are all high in carbohydrate.

Legumes, peas and beans including baked beans, lentils, kidney beans, chick peas etc.

Milk contains carbohydrate, in the form of milk sugar or lactose. Lactose is the first carbohydrate we encounter as infants. Use low-fat or skimmed milk and yoghurt to minimise fat intake.

SOURCES OF CARBOHYDRATE

Percentage of carbohydrate (grams per 100 grams of food) in food as eaten

apple	12%	peas	8%
baked beans	11%	pear	12%
banana	21%	plum	6%
barley	61%	potato	13%
bread	47%	rice	79%
cornflakes	85%	split peas	45%
flour	73%	sugar	100%
grapes	15%	sultanas	75%
ice cream	22%	sweet corn	16%
milk	5%	sweet potato	17%
oats	61%	tapioca	85%
orange	8%	water cracker	71%
pasta	70%	wheat biscuit	62%

INCLUDING LOW G.I. FOODS IN YOUR MEALS

Getting the benefits of low G.I. foods is easy. It just means making a few substitutions like those shown on the next page. Ideally, aim to swap at least half the foods you eat from a high G.I. to a low G.I. type. Perhaps you could change the type of bread or breakfast cereal and eat pasta or legumes more often.

Using any of the foods in this book will help you to lower the G.I. of your diet, but it isn't necessary to eat these foods alone. Normally, meals consist of a variety of foods, and we know that eating a low G.I. food with a high G.I. food produces an intermediate G.I.

To help yourself include low G.I. foods:
- become familiar with them (use this book)
- have them available in your kitchen cupboard (write a shopping list), and
- experiment with them (try new foods and recipes and enjoy what you eat)

A healthy, balanced diet contains a wide variety of low-fat, high carbohydrate foods.

SUBSTITUTING LOW G.I. FOR HIGH G.I. FOODS

High G.I. Food	Low G.I. Alternative
Bread, wholemeal or white	Bread containing a lot of 'grainy bits' such as multigrain or Ploughmans loaves
Processed breakfast cereal	Unrefined cereal such as rolled oats or muesli or a low G.I. processed cereal like All Bran™
Plain biscuits and crackers	Biscuits made with dried fruit and whole grains such as oats
Cakes and muffins	Make them with fruit, oats, whole grains
Tropical fruits such as bananas	Temperate climate fruits such as apples, stone fruit and citrus
Potato	Substitute with new potatoes, sweet potatoes, sweet corn and use more pasta and legumes
Rice	Try Basmati rice

STARCH AND THE G.I. FACTOR

Starch granules are composed of two types of starch molecule – a highly branched form called *amylopectin* and a straight chain form called *amylose*. The ratio of the two types of starch in the granule vary from one variety of food to another, and is genetically determined. Different varieties of corn and rice, for example, have different ratios of amylose to amylopectin.

Food processing alters starch granules, making them more readily digested. This is usually accomplished by heating in water (gelatinisation), but grinding may also be used. During cooking, heat and water make the starch granules swell so that the compact crystalline structure is destroyed. When making gravy with flour and water, the gradual thickening of the mixture corresponds to starch gelatinisation. Starches with higher amylose content swell more slowly and at higher temperatures because of stronger binding forces within the granules. In the case of very high amylose starches (such as we find in legumes), much of the amylose remains ungelatinised at the end of cooking and processing. As a result, there is restricted access by the digestive enzymes which delays overall digestion and absorption. In general, foods with a high ratio of amylose to amylopectin have lower G.I. factors.

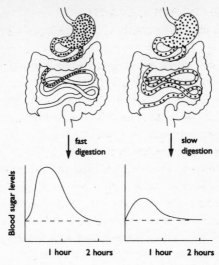

fast
digestion

slow
digestion

Blood sugar levels

1 hour   2 hours   1 hour   2 hours

Fast and slow carbohydrate digestion and the consequent levels of
sugar in the blood

The difference between raw (compact granules) and cooked (swollen
granules) starch in potatoes.

DID YOU KNOW ABOUT THE SUGAR–FAT SEESAW?

Did you know that fat and sugar tend to show a reciprocal or seesaw relationship in the diet? Studies over the past decade have found that diets high in sugar are no less nutritious than low sugar diets. This is because restricting sugar is frequently followed by higher fat consumption, and most fatty foods are poor sources of nutrients.

In some cases, high sugar diets have been found to have higher micronutrient contents. This is because sugar is often used to sweeten some very nutritious foods, such as yoghurts, breakfast cereals and milk.

A low sugar (and high fat) diet has more proven disadvantages than a high sugar (and low fat) diet.

ARE YOU REALLY CHOOSING LOW FAT?

There's a trick to food labels that it is worth being aware of when shopping for low fat foods. Nutrient claims are covered by food legislation that specifies what low fat really means.

Low fat means that the food must be 5% fat or less. On the nutrient table the food must not contain more than 5 g fat per 100 g food.

Reduced fat on the other hand means that the food must not contain more than 75% of the fat found in the original reference food. In other words, the amount of fat has to be reduced by at least 25% – but it isn't low enough in fat to be called a low fat food.

Where you have the choice, pick the low fat product. Better still is 'fat free' which contains less than 0.15% fat.

HOW TO USE THE A–Z LOW G.I. FOOD FINDER

This Food Finder tells you all about which foods have the lowest G.I. factors and why. Plus it has tips on how to enjoy these low G.I. foods.

INDEX TO YOUR LOW G.I. FOOD FINDER

Food	G.I. Factor	See Page
Frosties™	55	35
Muesli, natural	56	51
Porridge	42	65
Special K™	54	76
Sultana Bran™	52	78
Bush Foods		27
Cereal Grains		28
Barley	25	22
Bran, oat	55	55
Bran, rice	19	70
Buckwheat	54	25
Bulgur	48	26
Popcorn	55	64
Rye, whole kernel	34	83
Semolina	55	71
Wheat, quick cooking	54	68
Wheat, whole kernels	41	82
Dairy Foods		33
Custard	43	32
Ice cream, low-fat	50	41
Milk	30	50
Milk, skimmed	32	72
Yoghurt, low-fat, fruit	14–33	84

Food	G.I. Factor	See Page
Soy Drinks		
So Good™	31	72
Fruit		36
Apples	38	18
Apple juice	40	19
Apricots, fresh	57	19
Apricots, dried	31	34
Bananas	55	21
Cherries	22	30
Fruit cocktail	55	37
Grapefruit	25	38
Grapes	46	39
Kiwi fruit	52	43
Mangoes	55	49
Oranges	44	56
Orange juice	46	57
Pawpaw	58	58
Peaches	42	59
Pears	38	60
Pineapple juice	46	62
Plums	39	64
Sultanas	56	78
Legumes		45
Beans, baked	48	20
Beans, black-eyed	42	23
Beans, butter	31	28

Food	G.I. Factor	See Page
Beans, lima	32	46
Beans, haricot	38	53
Beans, kidney	27	42
Beans, navy	38	53
Beans, pinto	39	62
Beans, soy	18	74
Chick peas	33	30
Lentils	28(av)	45
Mung beans	38	52
Peas, dried	22	61
Peas, green	48	61
Peas, split	32	76
Pasta, Rice and Noodles		
Fettuccine	32	34
Macaroni	45	48
Noodles, instant	47	42
Noodles, Lungkow bean thread	26	47
Pasta		57
Ravioli	39	68
Rice, Basmati	58	22
Spaghetti	41	75
Tortellini	50	81
Vermicelli	35	82
Vegetables		81
Potatoes, new	78	53
Potatoes, canned	65	53

Food	G.I. Factor	See Page
Sweet corn	55	79
Sweet potato	54	79
Tomato soup, canned	38	80
Yam	51	84
Snack Foods and Drinks		
Chocolate	49	31
Honey	58	41
M&Ms™	33	48
Nutella™	33	55
Peanuts	14	58
Potato crisps	54	67
Sugars		
Fructose	23	35
Lactose	46	44

ALL-BRAN™ (KELLOGG)

G.I. Factor: 42

½ cup of All-Bran™ contains:

    22 g carbohydrate   1 g fat   9 g fibre

A good source of B-group vitamins and excellent source of insoluble fibre. All-Bran™ is made from coarsely milled wheat bran which has large pieces of endosperm (starch) still attached. This makes the starch less accessible to hydration and gelatinisation during processing and therefore to digest enzymes in the small intestine. The large pieces of bran form a physical barrier to enzymic attack while the large pieces of endosperm have a tightly packed, compact structure that is also resistant to digestion.

Eating tips: All-Bran™ has a malty taste and is good topped with sliced banana or canned pear slices and milk. Alternatively, sprinkle a few tablespoons over a lower fibre cereal to help meet your daily fibre requirement. All-Bran™ can also be added to cookies and muffins where it will boost the fibre content and lower the G.I. of the finished product.

APPLES

G.I. Factor: 38

A medium sized apple contains:

    20 g carbohydrate   0 g fat   3 g fibre

A crunchy, portable low G.I. snack which is a good source of fibre. Half the sugar in apples is fructose which has a very low G.I. Fructose is more slowly absorbed than glucose, and is only gradually converted to glucose in the liver. Apples are also high in malic acid (all acids slow down stomach emptying) and pectin (a soluble and viscous fibre that slows down the digestive process by increasing the viscosity of the intestinal contents). All these factors act together to make apples a low G.I. food.

Whole apples cause less secretion of the hormone insulin than apple puree or juice for reasons that are not entirely clear. Despite this, apple juice has a G.I. very close to whole apples. Cooking apples is likely to raise the G.I. slightly because it breaks down the cell wall barrier.

APPLE JUICE
G.I. Factor: 40
250 ml of unsweetened apple juice contains:
33 g carbohydrate   0 g fat   0 g fibre

Apple juice has a low G.I. attributable to its high fructose content.

APRICOTS
G.I. Factor: 57
2 medium apricots contain:
8 g carbohydrate   0 g fat   2.5 g fibre

Like apples, apricots are high in fructose (about half their carbohydrate) which contributes to their low G.I. The chewy, compact structure of the dried product probably limits access by digestive juices and explains the reduction in G.I. Canned apricots (G.I. = 64) have a similar G.I. to fresh apricots thus the process of canning in this case has little effect.

Apricots are available during the summer only, while dried apricots which have a particularly low G.I. (31) can be enjoyed as a healthy year-round snack. Cooking apricots draws out the flavour so they are delicious stewed. Apricots, like all orange-yellow plant foods, are a good source of carotenoids, a family of substances which contribute to vitamin A synthesis and have desirable anti-oxidant qualities. Apricots are also high in fibre and potassium.

BAKED BEANS
G.I. Factor: 48
½ cup of baked beans in tomato sauce contains:
   15 g carbohydrate   1 g fat   7 g fibre

A popular, ready-to-eat form of legumes. The digestibility of legumes is determined primarily by the nature of the starch which is entrapped in fibrous, thick-walled cells. This prevents the starch from swelling during cooking, lessening the degree of gelatinisation and reducing its digestibility. Baked beans are commonly made from haricot (navy) beans, which (like all legumes) have more amylose than cereal foods.

Home-cooked haricot beans have a lower G.I. factor (38) than baked beans. The process of canning plus the addition of sugar in the sauce raises the G.I., but not excessively. Canned baked beans are still a good low G.I. choice. Serve them on toast for a quick healthy meal.

BANANAS

G.I. Factor: 55

1 banana (18 cm) contains:

28 g carbohydrate   0 g fat   3 g fibre

A non-fattening carbohydrate snack which is a good source of fibre, many B vitamins plus vitamin C and potassium. Unlike most other fruits, bananas contain both starch and sugars (other fruits contain just sugars). The raw starch in bananas is not available for absorption and reaches the large bowel intact where it is fermented by the resident microflora. The products of fermentation are believed to be important for large bowel health and may reduce the risk of large bowel cancer. Cooking the banana gelatinises the starch, so that it becomes available for absorption and increases the G.I. As the banana ripens, the starch turns to sugars and the G.I. increases.

BARLEY

G.I. Factor: 25

½ cup of pearled barley, boiled, contains:

    20 g carbohydrate   1 g fat   3 g fibre

Pearled barley has had the outer brown layers of husk removed. It is very nutritious and high in fibre with one of the lowest G.I. factors of any food. Much of the fibre is a viscous, soluble fibre which helps to reduce the post-meal rise in blood glucose by increasing the viscosity of the intestinal contents. The higher the viscosity, the slower the mixing of enzymes and food. The near intact structure of the grain also keeps the G.I. low. Cook it as a porridge, eating with some milk and sugar or use it as you would rice. It can also be added to soups and stews.

BASMATI RICE

G.I. Factor: 58

½ cup of cooked basmati rice contains:

    25 g carbohydrate   0 g fat   1 g fibre

Basmati rice has a relatively low G.I. compared with other rices due to the high amylose nature of its starch (about 35% of the starch is amylose, compared to 0–25% of other varieties).

Basmati is a long grain rice with an aromatic flavour which develops with storage. The grains will stay firm and separate when cooked, a characteristic which reflects the compact structure of its starch. You can use this characteristic to guess the G.I. of rices eaten in restaurants. High amylose rices are preferred in Indian, Thai and Vietnamese cuisines while rices with less amylose have grains which tend to stick together when cooked, as preferred in Chinese cooking. The less amylose there is, the more sticky the grains will be and the higher the G.I. Rice desserts are often made from 'waxy' rice varieties that have no amylose at all and are very high on the G.I. scale (greater than 90).

BLACK-EYED BEANS
G.I. Factor: 42
½ cup of black-eyed beans contains:

    24 g carbohydrate   1 g fat   5 g fibre

Also known as black-eyed Suzies, black-eyed pea and southern pea. These are a small, kidney-shaped, creamy coloured bean with a distinctive black 'eye' and a subtle sweet flavour. Use them for soups and stews and in bean salads. A smaller glucose rise after legumes is explained by the relatively slow or incomplete break down of their starch. This is mainly due to containment of the starch in intact cell walls and also by its relatively high amylose content (see page 5). The presence in legumes of phenolic compounds (tannins and catechins), tends to slow down digestion by inhibiting the action of the amylase enzymes.

BRAN BUDS™
G.I. Factor: 58
30 g serving of Bran Buds™ contains:
14 g carbohydrate   1 g fat   5 g fibre

Another ready to eat high fibre cereal containing processed wheat bran and wheat starch – somewhat higher G.I. than All-Bran™, reflecting a different mixture of particle size, processing conditions and different proportions of slowly and rapidly digestible starch.

BREAD
One of the most important changes you can make to lower the G.I. of your diet is to choose a low G.I. bread. Choose heavy grain breads, such as the brands listed in this book, instead of the regular white, brown and whole-meal breads. Stone-ground wholemeal breads and white sourdough breads have a lower G.I. than conventional

bread. Breads which have been made by the traditional long fermentation process have low G.I. values. During this process, the yeast consumes the quickly digested starch converting it to energy, carbon dioxide (which makes the bread rise) and a little alcohol which evaporates during baking. What the yeast leaves behind is the more slowly digested starch which is our gain and their loss.

BREAD MIXED GRAIN
G.I. Factor: 34
1 slice of Bürgen™ Mixed Grain contains:
15g carbohydrate   2 g fat   2 g fibre

One of the most important changes you can make to lower the G.I. of your diet is to choose a low G.I. bread.

BUCKWHEAT
G.I. Factor: 54
½ cup of cooked buckwheat contains:
57 g carbohydrate   3 g fat   9 g fibre

A good source of protein, thiamin, niacin, iron and magnesium. Buckwheat is the seed of a herbaceous plant rather than a cultivated grass (cereal). It is often thought of as a cereal because it is used in the same manner and has a similar nutrient value. It can be cooked as a porridge or steamed and served with vegetables, in place of rice. It is also available ground, as buckwheat flour which is used for making pancakes (blini) and noodles (soba). The intact 'whole seed' structure accounts for the low G.I. because the seed coat limits access of digestive enzymes. Milling the seed to flour will result in a product with a higher G.I.

BULGUR
G.I. Factor: 48
½ cup of bulgur, boiled, contains:

23 g carbohydrate   0 g fat   6 g fibre

Bulgur is made by coarse grinding of dried cooked wheat grains and is popular in Middle Eastern cuisine. The parboiling and light crushing of the wheat grain in the process of making bulgur has only a small effect on the G.I. Bulgur is most commonly recognised as the main ingredient in Lebanese 'tabbouli', a mixture of parsley, bulgur, chopped tomato, onion and dressing. The compactness and intact physical form of the wheat contributes to its low G.I.

LOW G.I. EATING

Low G.I. eating means making a move back to the high carbohydrate foods which are staples in many parts of the world. The emphasis is on whole foods like whole grains – barley, oats, dried peas and beans, in combination with certain types of breads, pasta, rice, vegetables and fruits. Stock your pantry with these foods and keep a loaf of whole grain bread in the freezer. For recipes, check out our book, *The Glucose Revolution*, which includes more than 50 recipes specially modified to lower the G.I. plus new ways of preparing low G.I. food.

BUSH FOODS

Measurement of the G.I. factors of Australian Aboriginal bush foods has yielded some of the lowest G.I. figures of all. The flour made from acacia (wattle seeds), for example, has a G.I. of only 10. The fact that many staple, traditional foods have such low glycaemic indices gives rise to the hypothesis that they may have been protective against diabetes even in genetically susceptible individuals. Diabetes was not evident among Australian Aborigines until they adopted European diets and lifestyles. Now they have one of the highest rates of diabetes in the world. Some bush foods are available in

Australian supermarkets, and in Britain may occasionally be available in specialist shops in major cities.

BUTTER BEANS

G.I. Factor: 31

½ cup of butter beans contains:

15 g carbohydrate   0 g fat   5 g fibre

Butter beans are delicious in soups and the canned variety is useful to include as a vegetable on the dinner plate. The slow digestibility of legumes (such as butter beans) is determined by the nature of the starch which is entrapped in fibrous, thick-walled cells. This prevents the starch from swelling during cooking, lessening the degree of gelatinisation and reducing its digestibility. All legumes have more amylose than found in cereal grains.

CEREAL GRAINS

Cereal Grains are provided by nature in a slowly digested form. In early times, preparation involved rough grinding between stones, breaking the outer seed husk but leaving much of the grain intact. This limits gelatinisation of the starch during cooking and reduces the rate of digestion. The presence of antinutrients such as phytic acid, which occur naturally in cereal grains, further limited digestion. Today, cereal processing includes milling to fine flour, popping, toasting, flaking and extrusion cooking to make products such as cakes, breads, biscuits, snack products and breakfast cereals in which the starch is readily digested and the G.I. is high.

CHAPATI-BAISEN
G.I. Factor: 27
One chapati weighing 100 g contains:
44 g carbohydrate   1 g fat (made without oil)
3 g fibre

Chapati is an unleavened or slightly leavened bread, which resembles pitta bread in appearance. It is widely eaten in India and the Indian subcontinent. While it is often made with wheat flour, it is also made from baisen, or chick pea flour, which is milled from a small variety of chick peas. Chapati made from baisen has a significantly lower G.I. than that made from wheat flour, due to the nature of the starch. All legumes, including chick peas have a higher proportion of amylose starch than found in cereal grains.

CHERRIES

G.I. Factor: 22

10 cherries contain:

5 g carbohydrate   0 g fat   1 g fibre

A good source of potassium and vitamin C. Cherries have the lowest G.I. of any fruit according to a European study. We don't know exactly why this is the case but cherries have a somewhat 'rubbery' consistency, just like pasta and dried apricots, which is known to increase resistance to disruption in the intestine. Cherries are also acidic and high in sugars, both of which slow down the rate of stomach emptying and therefore digestion. Canned cherries in heavy syrup are likely to have a higher G.I. Fresh cherries are available for a relatively short season in early summer.

CHICK PEAS

G.I. Factor: 33

½ cup canned chick peas, drained, contains:

15 g carbohydrate   2 g fat   4 g fibre

A particularly versatile legume which is rich in protein, B group vitamins and minerals. Chick peas are the seed of a plant native to west Asia. Like all legumes they have an exceptionally low G.I. factor. The reasons include the encapsulation of the starch in a hard seed coat, a higher amylose ratio in the starch and the presence of substances that slow down digestion such as tannins and enzyme inhibitors that are not destroyed in the cooking process.

Prepare chick peas as you would other legumes, soaking and then boiling an hour to an hour and a half. Alternatively, use the canned varieties which have a slightly higher G.I. (42). Cooked or canned chick peas can be added to a tomato-curry based sauce to serve with couscous or rice. Soaked chick peas can be ground to a paste, mixed with spices and fried to make a Middle Eastern bean pattie, felafel. After soaking, whole chick peas can also be roasted with salt and spices to make a crunchy snack.

CHOCOLATE
G.I. Factor: 49
6 squares of milk chocolate (30 g) contains:
19 g carbohydrate   8 g fat   0 g fibre

Most people are surprised to learn that the world's favourite food has a relatively low G.I. Although half the weight is sugar, fat contributes most of the calories in chocolate. This much fat slows down stomach emptying so that the sugar reaches the small intestine gradually, and produces only a moderate rise in blood sugar levels, accounting for the low G.I. Other chocolate snacks such as M&Ms™ (G.I. = 33) and Snickers™ Bars (G.I. = 41) are also low G.I. foods, but they need to be eaten sparingly (one indulgence a day is OK) because of their high fat content. While most of the fat is saturated, much is in the form of stearic acid, a type of fat which has been shown to have a neutral effect on blood cholesterol levels (thank goodness!), so enjoy chocolate in moderation and walk the dog afterwards.

CUSTARD
G.I. Factor: 43
¾ cup of custard contains:

> 24 g carbohydrate   5 g fat (made with full cream milk)   0 g fibre

Prepared from commercial wheat starch with the addition of egg, milk and sugar. Its low G.I. may be explained by its fat content (which slows down stomach emptying) and its sugars – sucrose and lactose which have only half the glycaemic effect of pure wheat starch.

DAIRY FOODS

Lactose is the sugar found naturally in milk and milk products and is one reason behind their low G.I. (see Lactose). The presence of protein, fat and lactic acid in fermented milk products slows down stomach emptying and lowers the G.I. Low fat milk, yoghurt, ice cream and custard are recommended as excellent sources of calcium with a low G.I. Note, cheese (although another source of calcium) is not a source of carbohydrate, the lactose being drawn off in the whey during cheese manufacture.

DIGESTIVE BISCUITS

G.I. Factor: 59

2 plain digestive biscuits, 30 g, contain:

21 g carbohydrate   6 g fat   1.4 g fibre

Another biscuit – low G.I. because of the starch characteristics (see Rich Tea biscuits). However biscuits are energy dense and often have quite a lot of fat – note 6 g per portion here – that's 20% fat providing 180 kcal per 100 g or 54 kcal per 30 g portion. Low G.I., but easy to eat, therefore their use needs to be limited if you need to limit total dietary energy or fat intake.

DRIED APRICOTS
G.I. Factor: 31
5 apricot halves contain:
> *11 g carbohydrate   0 g fat   2.5 g fibre*

Excellent source of fibre and beta-carotene (the plant precursor of vitamin A). Also a source of iron. Makes a nourishing snack or addition to a school lunch box. The chewy compact structure of dried apricots probably limits access by digestive juices and explains the reduction in G.I. compared with fresh apricots. Half the sugars are in the form of fructose, which produces very little effect on blood sugar levels.

FETTUCCINE
G.I. Factor: 32
1 cup of boiled fettuccine contains:
> *57 g carbohydrate   1 g fat   3 g fibre*

Fettuccine is a ribbon shaped pasta, about 0.5 cm wide. It tastes great with cheese-based sauces but it is preferable to use tomato-based accompaniments that have only a fraction of the kilojoules. The reasons for its low G.I. are the same as those that apply to all pastas (see page 57).

FROSTIES™ (KELLOGG)
G.I. Factor: 55
¾ cup of Frosties™ contains:
> *27 g carbohydrate   0 g fat   1 g fibre*

We were very surprised to learn that Frosties™ had a relatively low G.I. factor. Most flaked cereals, whether high or low in sugar, have high G.I. values. In the case of Frosties™ it may be that the low water content and high sugar levels added during cooking (rather than afterwards) has resulted in limited gelatinisation of the starch. Ungelatinised starch granules take longer to be digested and therefore reduce the glycaemic effect. It just goes to show you that you can't guess the final G.I. of a food by examining the ingredient list.

FRUCTOSE
G.I. Factor: 23
Fructose (or fruit sugar) is a form of sugar that occurs naturally in all fruits and honey. Apples are a particularly rich source of free fructose. Fructose is also found as one half of the sucrose (refined sugar) molecule.

It is slowly absorbed into the blood stream and only gradually converted to glucose in the liver. Its presence in the liver brings about a prompt reduction in the body's normal glucose-producing mechanisms (something that glucose doesn't do). All in all, fructose has only 20% of the effect of pure glucose on blood sugar and insulin levels. Some studies show that very large amounts of fructose have undesirable effects on blood fats, but in normal everyday amounts that we find in most foods, there is no cause for concern.

FRUIT

The majority of fruits have a low G.I. The presence of sugars (especially fructose) which have low G.I. values, fibres (both soluble and insoluble) and acids (which may slow down stomach emptying) are probable reasons. Lowest G.I. fruits tend to be those grown in temperate climates such as apples, pears, citrus and stone fruit. The more acidic the fruit, the lower the G.I., e.g. grapefruit's G.I. is 25. Tropical fruits like melons, pineapple and bananas have intermediate G.I. factors. All fresh fruits are a source of vitamin C. Ideally several portions of fruit should be consumed each day.

FRUIT COCKTAIL
G.I. Factor: 55
Fruit cocktail canned in natural juice, 125 g, contains:
   15 g carbohydrate   0 g fat   2 g fibre

As expected, fruit cocktail has a glycaemic index reflecting the G.I. of its components, for example: apricots 57, peach 30, pear 44, cherry 22, pineapple 66, and the juices: pineapple 46, apple 40, etc.

FRUIT LOAF (CONTINENTAL)
G.I. Factor: 47
1 slice of regular fruit loaf contains:
   17 g carbohydrate   1 g fat   1 g fibre

The G.I. of fruit loaf is relatively low because of the part substitution of flour (high G.I.) with fruit (lower G.I.). The presence of sugar in the dough also limits gelatinisation of the starch in the flour, resulting in some ungelatinised starch granules that resist digestion in the small intestine. Fruit loaf makes a healthy between-meal snack, just as long as you spread the margarine thinly.

GRAPEFRUIT
G.I. Factor: 25
½ a grapefruit contains:

   5 g carbohydrate   0 g fat   0.5 g fibre

Half a grapefruit contains about 35 mg of vitamin C which almost equals a day's recommended intake. It is high in citric acid which lowers the G.I. by slowing down stomach emptying. Grapefruit are a refreshing food to eat and are popular at breakfast, halved and eaten as is or sprinkled with a little sugar. They can also be peeled and segmented and included as part of a winter fruit salad with sweeter fruits like oranges and raisins and a drizzle of honey. Grapefruit juice has a much higher G.I. (48) possibly because manufacturers endeavour to improve the palatability of the product by altering the acid:base balance, i.e. reducing the acidity using approved food additives.

GRAPES

G.I. Factor: 46

1 cup of green grapes contains:

    25 g carbohydrate   0 g fat   2 g fibre

Grapes have one of the highest sugar contents among temperate fruits. This is one reason they make a good starting product for alcoholic beverages (more sugar means more alcohol!). The high sugar content increases the 'osmolality' of the solution in the stomach (i.e. the osmotic pressure) and reduces the rate of stomach emptying which slows down digestion and absorption. Grapes are also quite high in acid, another factor which slows down the rate of food entering the small intestine.

DID YOU KNOW?

Most of the refined sucrose used in the manufacture of soft drinks, cakes and biscuits is not consumed as sucrose per se but as a mixture of glucose and fructose because time, heat and acid combine to split the molecule in two.

HIGHLAND OATMEAL BISCUITS
G.I. Factor: 55

2 Highland Oatmeal biscuits contain:
13 g carbohydrate   3 g fat   1 g fibre

Biscuit doughs have a low water:flour ratio and a high sugar content. This mix results in lower levels of starch gelatinisation than we find in bread. Ungelatinised starch granules are more resistant to enzyme attack in the small intestine. The presence of fat also tends to decrease starch gelatinisation as well as the rate of stomach emptying. All things considered, biscuits, whether high or low in sugar, are energy-dense and highly palatable foods that are easily overeaten. Go easy on them. Far better to have a slice of toasted low G.I. bread, spread with a smear of margarine and a dollop of jam.

HONEY
G.I. Factor: 58
One tablespoon, 20 g, of honey contains:
16 g carbohydrate   0 g fat   0 g fibre

Honey is basically a mixture of glucose (G.I. 100) and
fructose (G.I. 23) and has a G.I. close to that of sucrose –
a disaccharide composed of glucose and fructose (G.I.
60). Different tests on honey samples do give different
results probably reflecting different composition (many
honey products are blended).

ICE CREAM (LOW-FAT)
G.I. Factor: 50
2 level scoops (48 g) of reduced fat ice cream contains:
10 g carbohydrate   2 g fat   0 g fibre

Ice cream is a source of calcium. Look for low-fat or
reduced-fat ice creams when purchasing. Some taste as
good or better than their full fat counterpart. Ice cream
has a higher G.I. than milk alone because of the presence
of sucrose and glucose in addition to lactose. The mixture
of low and high G.I. sugars leads to an intermediate G.I.
product.

INSTANT NOODLES
G.I. Factor: 47
1 packet (80 g) of instant noodles contains:
55 g carbohydrate   16 g fat   1 g fibre

These Chinese-style dried noodles have become very popular as a quick meal or snack. They are a high carbohydrate convenience food but also contain a substantial amount of fat (over 35% of the kilocalories). The flavour sachets are based on salt and flavour enhancers (including monosodium glutamate). Keep them for occasional use, adding fresh or frozen chopped vegetables to make a quick meal. They can also be added to soups and stir-fries. Their low G.I. results from the dense physical structure that resists disruption in the small intestine in the same way that pasta does.

KIDNEY BEANS
G.I. Factor: 27
90 g of boiled kidney beans contains:
16 g carbohydrate   0.5 g fat   8 g fibre

There are so many varieties of the common bean *Phaseolus vulgaris*, and they are such important components of the low G.I. diet that they merit more than one entry. The varieties include haricot, navy, red kidney, cannelloni, marrow, flageolet and pea bean. They are not identical – the red kidney bean, for example, must be thoroughly cooked to inactivate the lectins in the seed coat (present to protect it from insect damage) – since undercooked red kidney beans can cause abdominal pain. Red kidney beans and other common bean varieties are major low G.I. sources of protein, energy and fibre for hundreds of millions of people across the globe.

KIWI FRUIT
G.I. Factor: 52
1 kiwi fruit contains:

      8 g carbohydrate   *0 g fat*   *3 g fibre*

An excellent source of vitamin C, with one kiwi fruit meeting the total recommended daily intake. Kiwi fruit contain equal proportions of glucose (high G.I.) and fructose (low G.I.) resulting in an intermediate G.I. They are also quite acidic fruits. Acids slow down stomach emptying and result in slower rates of digestion and absorption in the small intestine.

LACTOSE

G.I. Factor: 46

Lactose is a disaccharide which must be digested into its component sugars before absorption. The two sugars, glucose and galactose, compete with each other for absorption. Once absorbed galactose is mainly metabolised in the liver producing little effect on plasma glucose levels. Hence, ingestion of 50 g lactose is equivalent to consuming only 25 g glucose and the effect on blood glucose levels is proportionately lower.

For many years people with diabetes were advised to avoid all sugars, which for some, led to the restriction of milk, because of its lactose content. This is no longer considered necessary. Furthermore, milk is an important source of calcium throughout life. People of non-European ancestry are often lactose intolerant as teenagers and adults because the enzyme lactase is no longer active in their small intestine. This should not stop them from enjoying small amounts of milk in breakfast cereals, tea and coffee. They can also tolerate yoghurt even in large quantities because the micro-organisms in the yoghurt are active in digesting lactose during passage through the small intestine. Cheese is a good source of calcium, too, that is virtually free of lactose.

LEGUMES

Legumes are nature's lowest G.I. foods. The reasons include the encapsulation of the starch in a hard seed coat, a higher amylose ratio in the starch and the presence of substances that slow down digestion such as tannins and enzyme inhibitors that are not destroyed in the cooking process. They also contain starch which is totally resistant to digestion in the small intestine. Resistant starch behaves like fibre in the large bowel and may reduce the risk of developing colon cancer.

LENTILS
G.I. Factor: 28
½ cup dried lentils, boiled, contains:

9 g carbohydrate   0 g fat   3.5 g fibre

Lentils are one food that all people with diabetes should learn to love – you can eat them 'til the cows come home! We have found that no matter how much of them people eat, they have only a small effect on blood sugar levels. Lentils are rich in protein, fibre and B vitamins. They are often used as substitutes for meat in vegetarian recipes and associated with days of partial fasting in the Greek Orthodox church. The red lentil is one of the oldest known beans eaten by humans.

Green/brown lentils are also available. Both types have a similar, low, G.I., which is increased slightly by canning. They have a fairly bland, earthy flavour and are best prepared with onion, garlic and spices. Whole red lentils fade to yellow with cooking. They cook quickly to mush and are used to make Indian dahl (a spiced lentil puree) or curried lentil soup. They are also good for thickening any type of soup or extending meat casseroles. In winter, make a meal of lentil soup and low G.I. bread. You will feel thoroughly satisfied.

LIMA BEANS
G.I. Factor: 32
½ cup frozen, baby lima beans, contains:

17 g carbohydrate   0 g fat   6 g fibre

All legumes, including the lima bean, have a low G.I. The lima bean is a large variety of the butter bean. It has a floury texture and slightly sweet flavour. Baby lima beans can be boiled and served as vegetable alongside meat. Dried and canned lima beans can also be used in soups, stew, casseroles and salads. Legumes are nature's lowest G.I. foods. The reasons include the encapsulation of the starch in a hard seed coat, a higher amylose ratio in the starch and the presence of substances that slow down digestion such as tannins and enzyme inhibitors, that are not destroyed in the cooking process.

LUNGKOW BEAN THREAD NOODLES
G.I. Factor: 26
180 g Lungkow bean thread contains:

61 g carbohydrate   0 g fat   fibre (unavailable)

Also known as cellophane noodles or green bean vermicelli, these shiny, fine, white noodles are made from mung beans. They are usually sold in bundles, wrapped in cellophane in Asian supermarkets. They are simply soaked in hot water for 10 minutes to soften and can then be used in stir fries and salads. They tend to absorb the flavours of other foods they are cooked with. The reasons for their low G.I. include their legume origin (high proportion of amylose) and their noodle shape (dense texture).

M&MS™

G.I. Factor: 33

1 packet (60 g) of M&Ms™ contains:

38 g carbohydrate   15 g fat   3 g fibre

Although over half the weight is sugar, fat contributes most of the kilocalories in M&Ms™. This much fat slows down stomach emptying so that the sugar reaches the small intestine gradually, and produces only a moderate rise in blood sugar levels, accounting for the low G.I. Other chocolate products are also low G.I. foods, but all of them need to be eaten sparingly (one indulgence a day is OK) because of their high fat content. While most of the fat is saturated, much is in the form of stearic acid, a type of fat which has been shown to have a neutral effect on blood cholesterol levels.

MACARONI

G.I. Factor: 45

1 cup of boiled macaroni contains:

44 g carbohydrate   0 g fat   3 g fibre

All pastas have a low G.I. (40–50) whatever the shape and no matter how long you cook them. One reason for this is that the making of good pasta starts with wheat semolina (cracked wheat minus the bran) rather than flour. The larger the particle size of the cereal, the slower the rate of gelatinisation during cooking, and the slower the rate of digestion in the small intestine. Experiments also show that pasta made with flour tends to have a low G.I. The dense texture of all pasta products leads to less disruption during passage through the gastrointestinal tract. Pasta makes a quick and easy meal, with many freshly prepared pastas and sauces on the market (it's easy to make your own too). Stick to the tomato-based sauces rather than the creamy ones laden with fat, and use a modest sprinkling of cheese on top.

MANGOES
G.I. Factor: 55
1 mango contains:

    19 g carbohydrate   0 g fat   2 g fibre

Mango is one tropical fruit that squeezes into the low G.I. range. Most tropical fruits have a higher G.I. than temperate fruit, possibly related to differences in acidity and total solids (sugars). It is rich in naturally-occurring sugars, vitamin C and vitamin A precursors.

DID YOU KNOW ABOUT MARROWFAT PEAS?

Like all legumes, marrowfat peas have a low G.I. (39) and are very rich in all nutrients. The reasons for the low G.I. include the encapsulation of the starch in a hard seed coat, a higher amylose ratio in the starch and the presence of substances that slow down digestion such as tannins and enzyme inhibitors that are not destroyed in the cooking process. They are not widely available, but worth looking out for.

MILK
G.I. Factor: 30
1 cup (250 ml) of reduced fat milk contains:
   15 g carbohydrate   5 g fat   0 g fibre

Milk is a rich source of protein and vitamin B_2 (riboflavin). Unfortunately whole milk is a rich source of saturated fat, so it's preferable to consume reduced fat, low-fat and non-fat milk and milk products. The surprisingly low G.I. of milk results from the moderate glycaemic effect of the milk sugar (see Lactose) plus the effect of milk protein which forms a soft curd in the stomach and slows down the rate of stomach emptying.

Adding moderate amounts of refined sugar (e.g. in the form of chocolate syrup) does not alter the G.I. significantly. People who are lactose intolerant can find lactose-reduced milks on supermarket shelves (usually near the soy milks). Hot milk and honey makes a nutritious nightcap. Research shows that people do indeed sleep sounder after a milk drink at night. The active component is an amino acid called tryptophan which the body converts to serotonin, the hormone associated with calmness and well-being.

MUESLI, NATURAL
G.I. Factor: 56
½ cup (60 g) of natural muesli contains, (on average):

    32 g carbohydrate   6 g fat   7 g fibre

Muesli originated as a Swiss health food and nowadays rates as one of the few relatively unprocessed products on the market. It is a good source of carbohydrate, thiamin, riboflavin, and niacin. Beware of toasted versions that have been oven-baked with lots of added fat. This lowers the G.I. but doubles the kilocalories. The low G.I. results from the fact that the oats are eaten raw, and therefore in an ungelatinised state that resists digestion in the small intestine. Oats also contain a viscous fibre that increases the viscosity of the contents of the small intestine, thereby slowing down enzymic attack. This same fibre has also been shown to reduce blood cholesterol levels, but you need to eat more than an average serving to see this effect.

MUNG BEANS
G.I. Factor: 38
200 g of cooked mung beans *(Phaseolus aureus)* contains:
    36 g carbohydrate   1 g fat   20 g fibre

A small green bean that can be eaten with butter or spices or ground into a flour (cooking time 25–40 minutes). Like all legumes they are very nutritious and exceptionally low G.I. foods. Indian green gram dahl is a favourite ethnic dish based on mashed, cooked mung beans. They are a good source of dietary fibre, iron and protein. Sprouted mung beans are sold by the punnet and are a source of vitamin C.

NAVY/HARICOT BEANS
G.I. Factor: 38
½ cup dried navy haricot beans, boiled, contains:
> *11 g carbohydrate   1 g fat   8 g fibre*

These are the beans used for making baked beans. They are an excellent source of fibre, protein, iron, potassium and zinc. If you make your own baked beans, they'll have a lower G.I. than the canned variety. Legumes of all sorts, including navy beans, are renowned for producing flatulence (gas) and many jokes. The components responsible are indigestible sugars called raffinose, stachyose and verbascose. They reach the large bowel intact where they are fermented by the resident microflora. Believe or not, this is good for colonic health, increasing the proportion of good *Bifidobacteria* and reducing the potential pathogens.

NEW POTATOES, CANNED
G.I. Factor: 62
A 60 g new potato, boiled, contains:
> *8 g carbohydrate   0 g fat   1 g fibre*

Most potatoes have a high G.I. but small new potatoes appear to be the exception. In fact, we found that the smaller the potato, the lower the G.I. Canned potatoes are the smallest, followed by fresh new potatoes (G.I. = 78). They are also known as chats or cocktail potatoes. They are good to steam, boil or include in a potato salad. The relatively low G.I. (compared with the mature potato) results from the lack of branching in the amylopectin starch. As the potato matures and grows bigger, the amylopectin becomes increasingly branched making it easier to gelatinise during cooking. The branching of the molecule increases the openness of the granules and inhibits bonding between chains of starch. Water is absorbed more easily and the starch granule swells (gelatinises) at lower temperatures. Gelatinised starch granules are easier to digest because the enzymes can gain quick access.

NUTELLA™
G.I. Factor: 33
1 tablespoon (20 g) contains:

      12 g carbohydrate   6 g fat   fibre (unavailable)

Nutella™ is a sweetened chocolate spread based on hazel-nuts that most children love. The fat content is high but it is mainly mono- and poly-unsaturated fat and there-fore a healthy addition to the diet of active youngsters. (**NB** Low-fat diets are not suitable for young children.) The low G.I. of Nutella™ results from the rich mixture of fat and sugars – high concentrations of both slow down stomach emptying.

OAT BRAN
G.I. Factor: 55
1 tablespoon of raw oat bran contains:

      6 g carbohydrate   1 g fat   2 g fibre

Unprocessed oat bran is available in the cereal section of health food shops, usually loosely packed in plastic bags. Its carbohydrate content is lower than that of oats and it is higher in fibre, particularly soluble fibre, which is responsible for its low G.I. When mixed with water, oat bran forms a jelly-like mixture that increases the viscosity of the solution in the small intestine. This slows down the movement of enzymes and food, resulting in slower rates of digestion. A soft, bland product, oat bran is a useful addition to breakfast cereals and as a partial substitution for flour in baked goods to lower the G.I.

ORANGES
G.I. Factor: 44
1 orange contains:

10 g carbohydrate   0 g fat   3 g fibre

Special benefits: Oranges and orange juice are major contributors to vitamin C intake. One orange can provide around 60 mg of vitamin C, the whole day's requirement.

Much of the sugar content of oranges is sucrose, a 'double' sugar made up of glucose and fructose. When digested, only the glucose molecule makes an impression on blood sugar levels. This and their high acid content, account for their low G.I.

ORANGE JUICE

G.I. Factor: 46

1 cup (250 ml) unsweetened orange juice contains:

   21 g carbohydrate   0 g fat   1 g fibre

Processed orange juice contains approximately equal amounts of fructose, glucose and sucrose because much of the original sucrose is partially split ('hydrolysed') to glucose and fructose during processing.

PASTA

Most pasta is made from *semolina* (cracked wheat) which is milled from very hard wheat with a high protein content. Durum wheat is a hard, high protein wheat that is considered to make the best pasta. A stiff dough is made by mixing the semolina with water which is forced through a die and dried. There is minimal mechanical disruption of the starch granule during this process and strong protein-starch interactions inhibit starch gelatinisation. The dense consistency also makes the pasta resistant to disruption in the small intestine and contributes to the final low G.I. – even pasta made from fine flour instead of semolina has a relatively low G.I. There is some evidence that thicker pasta has a lower G.I. than thin types for this reason. The addition of egg to fresh pasta lowers the G.I. by increasing the protein content. Higher protein levels inhibit stomach emptying.

PAWPAW
G.I. Factor: 58
Half a small pawpaw, 200 g, contains:

11 g carbohydrate   0 g fat   3 g fibre

High in carotene and vitamin C (60 mg/100 g) pawpaw, or papaya, originated in middle America, but is now widely available throughout the tropical world where it is grown and as an imported fruit in Western countries. The sugar content is 3% glucose (G.I. 100), 3% sucrose (G.I. 60) and 3% fructose (G.I. 23) – giving an average G.I. of 61. In the whole fruit the G.I. of 61 is lowered to 58, probably by the physical structure of the fruit.

PEANUTS
G.I. Factor: 14
½ cup of roasted, salted peanuts contains:

11 g carbohydrate   41 g fat   5 g fibre

A low carbohydrate but high fat, high protein food (50% fat and 25% protein). They grow under the ground (alias ground nut) and are used as a source of oil. They are also an excellent source of vitamins E and B complex. They are so low in carbohydrate that their G.I. doesn't really count although their high fat content does. They are easy to overconsume, so give yourself a specific ration. All processed peanuts are screened for the presence of fungus that produces a toxin called aflatoxin, one of the most carcinogenic substances known. Shelled peanuts are not screened so be careful never to eat a mouldy one by mistake.

PEACHES
G.I. Factor: 42
1 medium peach contains:

    9 g carbohydrate   0 g fat   2 g fibre

Much of the sugar in peaches is sucrose (4.7%), which is identical to normal table sugar. It is a 'double' sugar made up of glucose and fructose. When digested, only the glucose molecule makes an impression on blood sugar levels. This fact, their soluble fibre content and their natural acidity account for their low G.I. Peaches canned in heavy sugar syrup have a substantially higher G.I. factor (= 58) because refined sugar (G.I. = 65) makes up a larger proportion of the sugars and does not carry the same concentration of fibre or organic acids. Peaches canned in natural juice have a G.I. of only 30, perhaps because the final product has a higher osmolality (osmotic pressure) that slows down stomach emptying.

PEARS
G.I. Factor: 38
1 pear contains:

    23 g carbohydrate   0 g fat   4 g fibre

Pears have a high content of fructose (6.7%), a sugar which has minimal effect on blood sugars. Unlike peaches, the G.I. of canned pears (44) is virtually the same as the fresh product.

Pears are at their peak during autumn. They ripen quickly and should be eaten before they get too soft. They are a nice accompaniment to cheese and walnuts on a platter for dessert. They also make a stylish dessert poached or baked in a syrup or red wine.

PEAS, GREEN
G.I. Factor: 48

½ cup of green peas contains:

    5 g carbohydrate   0 g fat   5 g fibre

Peas are properly classified as legumes. They are high in fibre and also higher in protein than most other vegetables. More amylose, lower degrees of starch gelatinisation and protein-starch interactions may contribute to their lower G.I. While most of the carbohydrate is starch, they also average 3.5% sucrose giving them a sweet flavour.

PEAS, DRIED
G.I. Factor: 22

½ cup of dried green peas contains:

    4 g carbohydrate   0 g fat   3.5 g fibre

Also known as blue peas, but they are actually a pale, greenish colour and properly classified as legumes. The traditional peas used to make the old English pease pudding or mushy peas were blue peas. They take about 1 hour to cook after soaking and tend to disintegrate if overcooked, hence the name of the dish, 'mushy peas'. Their low G.I. derives from a combination of factors –

higher amylose content, physical entrapment of starch inside the cell wall of the seed, lower levels of starch gelatinisation during cooking and higher levels of substances that inhibit enzymes (such as tannins).

PINEAPPLE JUICE
G.I. Factor: 46

1 cup (250 ml) unsweetened pineapple juice contains:
   27 g carbohydrate   0 g fat   0 g fibre

The low G.I. factor of pineapple juice may be attributable to its acidity and high sugar content, which reduces the rate of stomach emptying. Fresh pineapple juice is a good source of vitamin C, but levels are significantly reduced by canning.

PINTO BEANS
G.I. Factor: 39

90 g pinto beans, soaked and boiled contains:
   21 g carbohydrate   0.6 g fat   8 g fibre

Another variety of the common bean *Phaseolus vulgaris*, the dried pinto bean is packed with protein (22%), energy as carbohydrate (50%), and vitamins E and B. It contains little fat, hence the use of dried beans as an important readily stored food in many cultures.

PITTA BREAD
G.I. Factor: 57
1 medium sized (24 cm diameter) pitta bread contains:
50 g carbohydrate   2 g fat   3 g fibre

Unleavened flat bread was found to have a lower G.I. than regular bread in a Canadian study. Pitta bread is sold prepacked in supermarkets. The lower G.I. may result from a denser food matrix that resists digestion in the small intestine compared with the light airy texture of leavened bread.

PLOUGHMAN'S WHOLEGRAIN LOAF
G.I. Factor: 47
1 slice of Wholegrain Loaf contains:
21 g carbohydrate   1 g fat   3 g fibre

A wholemeal bread made with a mixture of flour and soft-ened whole grains (kibble) which is often available in supermarkets. A similar product sold without the 'grainy bits' has a higher G.I. (64).

PLUMS
G.I. Factor: 39
1 plum contains:

     5 g carbohydrate   *0 g fat*   *1 g fibre*

The combination of organic acids and high concentration of sugar in plums slows down the rate of stomach emptying thereby reducing the glycaemic response. Plums also contain viscous fibre which reduces the rate of digestion in the small intestine.

POPCORN (MICROWAVE – LOW-FAT)
G.I. Factor: 55
1 cup of commercial popcorn contains:

     4 g carbohydrate   *2 g fat*   *1 g fibre*

Microwave popcorn has less than 10% fat in the final product compared with almost 30% in most varieties. It is more difficult to find on supermarket shelves. Popcorn is made from a special type of corn in which high heat causes the kernels to expand with steam and burst open exposing the starchy centre of the grain. It has a surprisingly low G.I. considering that popping gives other products a very high G.I. (e.g. Rice Pops, G.I. = 83). Low moisture in the starting product may inhibit starch gelatinisation. Popcorn contains a reasonable amount of fibre and can be low in fat (depending on preparation).

PORRIDGE
G.I. Factor: 42
1 cup of cooked rolled oats contains:

> *22 g carbohydrate   3 g fat   3 g fibre*

Porridge is a good source of viscous soluble fibre, B group vitamins, vitamin E, iron and zinc. Published G.I. factors range from 42 for ordinary porridge oats, to as high as 66 for 'one-minute oats'. Differences in milling, pre-cooking, degree of gelatinisation and soluble fibre content may explain the range of values. Rolled oats are hulled, steamed and flattened oats while oatmeal contains small particles of whole grain oats ground into a semi-fine grit. The additional flaking of rolled oats to produce quick cooking oats increases the rate of digestion causing a higher G.I. Supplementing a low fat diet with rolled oats can add a further cholesterol lowering effect. Don't be afraid to add a little brown sugar and milk to increase your enjoyment of porridge.

POTATOES – WHICH TO CHOOSE

Boiled, mashed, baked or chipped – everyone loves potatoes in some form or another and they're a good source of fibre and vitamin C. Unfortunately, most potatoes have high G.I. values. The only potatoes found to bear anything close to a low G.I. were the tiny, new, canned variety (G.I. = 65). The lower G.I. of new potatoes may be due to differences in the structure of the starch. As potatoes age, the degree of branching of their amylopectin starch increases significantly, becoming more readily gelatinised, digested and thus producing a higher G.I. New potatoes are also smaller than mature potatoes and a correlation has been found between the size of the potato and its G.I. factor – the smaller the potato the lower the G.I.

So, we suggest, eat small, new potatoes for preference. Combine your favourite potatoes with low G.I. foods like sweet corn, legumes, low G.I. breads, or even fruits and dairy in dessert. Put the low G.I. focus on the other meals in your day. Vary your diet with other sources of carbohydrate – rice, pasta, legumes. And, remember, potatoes are fat free, nutritious and very satisfying and not everything has to have a low G.I. – so enjoy them!

POTATO CRISPS
G.I. Factor: 54

A 50 g bag of potato crisps contains:

24 g carbohydrate   16 g fat   3 g fibre

A high fat, high salt snack food. A 50 g packet has the same kilocalories as nearly 4 slices of bread. The large surface area of the chip allows maximum uptake of the fat they are cooked in – usually palm oil (a saturated fat which should be kept to a minimum in our diet). Keep potato crisps for the occasional snack and buy the brands which use unsaturated fat. Most 'lite' potato crisps are not lower in fat but 'lightly' salted.

PUMPERNICKEL BREAD
G.I. Factor: 50

1 slice (60 g) of pumpernickel bread contains:

21 g carbohydrate   1 g fat   5 g fibre

Also known as rye kernel bread because the dough it is made from contains 80 to 90% whole and cracked rye kernels. It has a strong flavour and is usually sold thinly sliced. The main reason for its low G.I. is its content of whole cereal grains. Bread made from whole wheat grains would be expected to have a similarly low G.I.

QUICK COOKING WHEAT
G.I. Factor: 54

¼ of cup of whole wheat contains:

    25 g carbohydrate   2 g fat   9 g fibre

Whole wheat grains which have been physically treated to induce numerous small fissures, which allow rapid hydration and short cooking times. Its whole grain physical structure decreases gelatinisation and therefore accessibility of enzymes to the starch. There may also be some amylase inhibitor activity remaining in the germ of the wheat grain.

RAVIOLI
G.I. Factor: 39

1 cup of commercial ravioli (meat filled) contains:

    37 g carbohydrate   13 g fat   4 g fibre

Usually bought fresh or vacuum packed, with a huge variety of fillings available. A home-made tomato soup topped with floating ravioli and grated Parmesan cheese makes a delicious, low G.I. meal.

RED KIDNEY BEANS
G.I. Factor: 27 (home-cooked)
52 (canned beans)

½ cup canned red kidney beans contains:

12 g carbohydrate   0.5 g fat   6 g fibre

Red kidney beans are widely used in South America and are popular in Australia in dishes like chilli con carne and Mexican tacos and burritos. Traditionally, dried beans are soaked overnight and then cooked for 2 hours in boiling water. We tend to eat more beans in the canned form which has a higher G.I. (=52) than beans prepared by traditional methods (=27). The high temperatures and/or pressures of the canning process soften the seed casing and induce greater degrees of starch gelatinisation, making it more accessible to digestive enzymes. Nonetheless, canned kidney beans are low G.I. foods, high in fibre and protein and make a valuable addition to a diet.

RICE BRAN

G.I. Factor: 19

1 tablespoon of rice bran contains:

2 g carbohydrate   2 g fat   2 g fibre

Good source of thiamin, riboflavin and niacin with a sweet malty flavour.

Rice bran is the outer bran layer scraped from brown rice in the milling of white rice. It contains the fibrous seed coat and a small part of the germ. It is rich in fibre (25% by weight) and oil (20% by weight) and has an extremely low G.I. Rice bran is available in some health food shops. Sprinkle it on breakfast cereal or add to baked goods or meat loaf.

RICH TEA BISCUITS

G.I. Factor: 55

2 Rich Tea biscuits contain:

16 g carbohydrate   3 g fat   1 g fibre

Biscuit doughs have a low water:flour ratio and a high sugar content. This mix results in lower levels of starch gelatinisation than in bread. All things considered, biscuits, whether high or low in sugar, are energy-dense and highly palatable foods that are easily overeaten. Go easy on them. Far better to have a slice of toasted low G.I. bread or fruit loaf, spread with a smear of margarine and/or a dollop of jam.

SALAD VEGETABLES

Salad vegetables such as tomatoes, lettuce, cucumber, peppers and onions have so little carbohydrate that it's impossible to test their G.I. (50 g carbohydrate portions would be 1–2 kg worth!). In generous serving sizes, they will have no effect on blood sugars and should be regarded as 'free' foods that are full of desirable micronutrients.

SEMOLINA
G.I. Factor: 55
1 cup of semolina contains:
> *17 g carbohydrate   0 g fat   0 g fibre*

Semolina is the coarsely milled inner part of the wheat grain called the 'endosperm'. It is granular in appearance. Durum wheat semolina is used for making pasta. It can be bought in the cereal section of supermarkets and cooked and eaten as a porridge. It is also sold as instant flour or gravy flour, marketed for thickening sauces and gravies. It can be shaken straight into hot liquid for instant thickening. The large particle size (compared with fine wheat flour) limits starch gelatinisation and results in slower rates of digestion.

SKIMMED MILK
G.I. Factor: 32
250 ml of skimmed milk contains:

    13 g carbohydrate   0 g fat   0 g fibre

The pattern of use of milk in the UK has changed dramatically over the last 30 years. Full fat milk (G.I. 27) providing 10 g fat per 250 ml serving is used much less than semi-skimmed (reduced fat) milk (G.I. 30) providing 5 g fat per 250 ml serving [See page 50]. Skimmed milk is now widely used.

SO GOOD™
G.I. Factor: 31
1 cup of So Good™ contains:

    12 g carbohydrate   9 g fat   0 g fibre

If you use soy milk in preference to cows' milk, always check that it is enriched with calcium. So Good™ has the same calcium content as cows' milk and can be used any time in place of milk – as a drink or in recipes. Using soy milk is one way of increasing your intake of soy foods and obtaining the benefits of soy beans (see below).

SOURDOUGH RYE BREAD
G.I. Factor: 57
One slice, 50 g, of sourdough rye bread contains:

     23 g carbohydrate   2 g fat   3 g fibre

Rye is an important cereal crop in cooler parts of northern Europe where it grows well on poor soils. However it has poor bread-making qualities so is often mixed with wheat flour in which the protein quality and amount is more conducive to development of a lighter 'crumb'. In the absence of wheat a sourdough process involving lactic acid fermentation is sometimes used, to generate bread with better characteristics.

SOY & LINSEED LOAF

G.I. Factor: 19

1 slice of Soy & Linseed Loaf contains:

18 g carbohydrate   *4 g fat*   *5 g fibre*

One of the lowest G.I. foods yet discovered. Has the added benefits of soybeans and linseeds which contain phytoestrogens (a plant form of oestrogen) that have been shown to relieve the symptoms of menopause. Because these ingredients contain a reasonable amount of fat, this variety of bread contains the most fat. This shouldn't deter you from enjoying it (unless you are on a very low-fat diet) because the type of fat present is unsaturated and rich in omega-3 fatty acids (i.e. the good essential oils).

SOY BEANS

G.I. Factor: 18

½ cup canned soya beans contains:

2 g carbohydrate   *5.5 g fat*   *5 g fibre*

Very good source of fibre, iron, zinc and vitamin B. Soy beans are an excellent source of protein and have been a staple food in Asian countries for thousands of years. They are also higher in fat than other legumes, but the majority of this is polyunsaturated. They are quite low in carbohydrate. Soy beans also contain phyto-oestrogens (a type of plant oestrogen similar in structure to the female hormone oestrogen, but with a much weaker action). Many studies associate soy beans with beneficial effects – improvements in blood cholesterol levels, alleviation of menopausal symptoms, lower risk of breast cancer. Two to three servings of soy per day are needed to achieve these benefits. Canned soy beans appear to have a similar G.I. to the home-cooked counterpart.

Eating tips: Soy beans can be purchased dried (need to be soaked and then boiled for about 2 hours) or canned. May also be consumed as soy bean curd (tofu), soy bean flour, tempeh, miso, or textured vegetable protein (TVP), all of which have little carbohydrate and therefore minimal effect on blood sugar levels.

SPAGHETTI
G.I. Factor: 41
1 cup of cooked spaghetti contains:

56 g carbohydrate   1 g fat   3 g fibre

Spaghetti is probably the most popular pasta. It is well known in Spaghetti Bolognese but also makes a delicious dish tossed with fresh chopped herbs, minced garlic and a little olive oil. Spaghetti, like all pasta has a low G.I. because the starting product is a dough made from high protein semolina (large particles of wheat) and, secondly, because of its dense food matrix that resists disruption in the small intestine. Both fresh or dried spaghetti have a low G.I. Canned spaghetti, which is usually made from flour rather than semolina, and is very well cooked – has a higher G.I.

SPECIAL K™ (KELLOGG)
G.I. Factor: 54
1 cup of Special K™ contains:

  21 g carbohydrate 0 g fat 1 g fibre

Special K™ has twice the protein content (20%) of normal breakfast cereals. This factor slows down the rate of stomach emptying, thereby reducing the rate of starch digestion and absorption.

SPLIT PEAS, YELLOW, DRIED, COOKED
G.I. Factor: 32
½ cup dried split peas, cooked, contains:
6 g carbohydrate   0 g fat   3.5 g fibre

Split peas are prepared from a variety of the common garden pea with the husk removed. They may be yellow or green. Indian yellow split peas are used to make a dhal known as gram dhal or chana dhal. These split peas, known as channa, are smaller than the normal version and have a nutty flavour. Your local Indian take-away will sell prepared dhals. Combined with flat bread, lightly cooked vegetables and Basmati rice, they make a delicious low G.I. meal.

SPONGE CAKE
G.I. Factor: 46
A 60 g slice of plain sponge cake contains:
32 g carbohydrate   4 g fat   1 g fibre

Although sponge cake ranks moderately amongst cakes for fat content, it is very high in cholesterol because it is based on eggs. On an occasional basis, it is a good choice of cake for a low-fat diet, providing it is eaten with a low-fat topping. The low G.I. of sponge cake results from the low degree of starch gelatinisation in the presence of high amounts of sugar.

SULTANA BRAN™
G.I. Factor: 52

45 g serving of Sultana Bran™ contains:

35 g carbohydrate   1 g fat   7 g fibre

The glycaemic index of this mixed wheat bran and dried fruit product demonstrates the effects of mixtures. The G.I. of the mixture is slightly lower than that of sultanas (54) as a consequence of the lower G.I. of processed bran products (the other component). A good source of insoluble fibre – an ideal component of breakfast or of a late evening snack.

SULTANAS
G.I. Factor: 56

1 tablespoon of sultanas contains:

14 g carbohydrate   0 g fat   3 g fibre

Sultanas are less acidic than grapes and this may account for their slightly higher G.I. High acidity is associated with lower G.I. because the acid slows down stomach emptying. Use in cakes, biscuits, scones, as a sweetener on breakfast cereal and as a low G.I. snack.

SWEET CORN
G.I. Factor: 55
½ cup of corn kernels or 1 cob (5 cm long) contains:
18 g carbohydrate   1 g fat   3 g fibre

Excellent source of fibre and popular vegetable with children. Always buy fresh corn with the husk intact for the best flavour, because the sugar in the kernels transforms into starch the moment the husk is removed. Fresh, frozen or canned varieties are all suitable but corn-on-the-cob has a lower G.I. than corn chips or cornflakes. The intact whole kernel makes enzymic attack more difficult.

SWEET POTATO
G.I. Factor: 54
½ cup of mashed sweet potato contains:
20 g carbohydrate   0 g fat   2 g fibre

The orange coloured sweet potato (kumara) is an excellent source of beta-carotene, the plant precursor of vitamin A. Sweet potato is also a good source of vitamin C and fibre. The sweet flavour comes from naturally present sucrose (3%) which increases during storage in warm climates to as much as 6%. The low G.I. is associated with increased amounts of amylose.

Sweet potato is a traditional Pacific Island food which is now popular in Australia. It belongs to a different plant family to regular potato and has a much lower G.I. Prepare and cook as for ordinary potato – steaming, boiling, baking or frying. It is also tasty used in casseroles, curries and soups.

TOMATO SOUP
G.I. Factor: 38
1 cup (250 ml) of canned tomato soup, prepared, contains:

19 g carbohydrate   2 g fat   1 g fibre

Canned tomato soups contain large amounts of sodium so look for salt-reduced varieties when purchasing. Besides making an easy meal with some low G.I. toast, tomato soup can be used undiluted as a casserole or Bolognese sauce base. The low G.I. is related to its acidity and the bulk of its carbohydrate being sucrose.

TORTELLINI
G.I. Factor: 50
180 g of cheese tortellini contains:
21 g carbohydrate   8 g fat   1 g fibre

Small, crescent-shaped filled pasta. The range of fillings is unlimited, with examples being spinach and ricotta, chicken and veal, ham and cheese. Tortellini is usually bought fresh, or vacuum packed, boiled and then served with a sauce or just grated cheese. The nutrient content will vary depending on the type of filling. Like all pasta, tortellini have a low G.I.

VEGETABLES
You can eat most vegetables without thinking about their G.I. At least 4 servings of different vegetables should be eaten daily. Most are so low in carbohydrate that they have no measurable effect on our blood sugar levels but they still provide valuable amounts of fibre, vitamins and minerals. Higher carbohydrate vegetables include potato, sweet potato and sweet corn (strictly speaking corn is a cereal). Amongst these, sweet corn and sweet potato are the lowest G.I. choices. Pumpkin, carrots, peas and beetroot contain some carbohydrate but a normal serving size

contains so little that it does not raise our blood sugar levels significantly. Eat and enjoy!

VERMICELLI
G.I. Factor: 35
1 cup of cooked vermicelli (180 g) contains:
> *45 g carbohydrate   1 g fat   0 g fibre*

A thinner version of spaghetti which is good in soups and with stir-fries. Because it is so fine it cooks quickly in boiling water. Vermicelli was tested on a product made with durum wheat semolina, enriched with egg. Both these aspects and the spaghetti shape contribute to its low G.I.

WHOLE WHEAT KERNELS
(SOAKED IN WATER AND COOKED)
G.I. Factor: 41
50 g of whole wheat contains:
> *31 g carbohydrate   1 g fat   5 g fibre*

This is the wheat version of rice but takes much longer to cook. Greek foods with special religious significance are made from cooked wheat kernels mixed with sugar and spices. The outer bran layer inhibits water absorption during cooking and limits starch gelatinisation, thereby ensuring a low G.I. Phytic acid in the wheat has been shown to reduce starch digestibility as well. Milling to flour increases the G.I. markedly, depending on the final particle size. Stone ground flour has a lower G.I. than normal flour.

WHOLE KERNEL RYE
G.I. Factor: 34
50 g of whole kernel rye contains:
   33 g carbohydrate   1 g fat   6 g fibre

Whole kernel rye is used to make rye breads, pumpernickel bread and some crisp breads. It is an excellent source of fibre and also a good source of vitamins and minerals. It is rarely sold as such, but is available as rye flakes which are hulled, steamed and rolled rye grains. Like rolled oats, they can be cooked and eaten as a porridge. The intact grain structure limits the access of digestive enzymes and slows digestion of the starch, giving the final product a low G.I.

YAM

G.I. Factor: 51

100 g of yam contains:

    32 g carbohydrate   0 g fat   4 g fibre

Good source of vitamin C and potassium. Yams are the edible roots of climbing plants of many species. They are similar to sweet potato and can be prepared in a similar way – boiled, baked, deep fried. Australian Aborigines used many species of yam as staple foods. They were protected from diabetes as long as they led a traditional lifestyle and ate bush tucker. Unfortunately, modern foods are associated with a marked risk of diabetes in this population. The low G.I. is related to a higher proportion of amylose in the starch fraction.

YOGHURT, LOW-FAT FRUIT

G.I. Factor: 14–33

A 200 g tub of low fat yoghurt contains:

    14 g carbohydrate (artificially sweetened 'Diet')
    25 g carbohydrate (sugar sweetened)
    0 g fat   0 g fibre

Yoghurt is a concentrated milk product and rich in calcium, riboflavin and protein. Low-fat natural yoghurt provides the most calcium for the least kilocalories (520 mg of calcium for a 200 g tub). In the making of yoghurt, the bacterial culture added to milk breaks down some of the lactose into lactic acid which denatures the protein and forms a soft curd. The acidity and high protein content slow down stomach emptying contributing to the low G.I. value. Lactose, the sole carbohydrate in the unsweetened product, has a low G.I. by itself (= 46). In fruit yoghurts (G.I. = 33), the addition of sugar-sweetened fruit syrup mixture increases their G.I. over that of an artificially sweetened yoghurt (G.I. = 14). Lactose-intolerant people can safely consume yoghurt containing live cultures without fear of symptoms. Special types of bacteria added to some yoghurts (e.g. *Bifidobacteria*) may colonise the large intestine and convey health benefits. Research in this area, however, is still controversial.

SUSTAINING LOW G.I. SNACKS

Try a muffin

A smoothie

Raisin toast

A juicy orange

A mini-can of baked beans

A bowl of bran flakes with low-fat milk

A piece of pitta bread and Marmite™

A small tub of low-fat yoghurt

A sandwich

Dried apricots

A handful of sultanas

A big green apple

Low-fat ice cream in a cone

A pile of popcorn (low fat of course)

WHERE TO GO FOR HELP AND FURTHER INFORMATION

If you would like further information about a food and its glycaemic index, write to us, enclosing a stamped, self-addressed envelope. Address your letter to:

Associate Professor Jennie Brand-Miller
Human Nutrition Unit
Department of Biochemistry
University of Sydney NSW 2006.
Fax: 61 (02) 9351 6022
We welcome your feedback!

Information on the glycaemic index can also be obtained through dietitians and Diabetes UK. Contact the National Office for a local service.

British Dietetic Association
5th Floor, Elizabeth House
22 Suffolk Street
Queensway
Birmingham, B1 1LS
Tel: 0121 616 4900

British Diabetic Association
10 Queen Anne Street
London, W1M 0BD
Tel: 0207 323 1531

Irish Nutrition & Dietetic Institute
Dundrum Business Centre
Frankfort Dundrum
Dublin 14
Ireland
Tel: (1) 298 7466

ABOUT THE AUTHORS

Kaye Foster-Powell, an accredited practising dietitian-nutritionist, has extensive experience in diabetes management and has researched practical applications of the glycaemic index. She is the senior dietitian at Wentworth Area Diabetes Service and conducts a private practice in the Blue Mountains, NSW.

Jennie Brand-Miller is Associate Professor of Human Nutrition in the Human Nutrition Unit at the University of Sydney. She is a world authority on the glycaemic index of foods and its applications to health.

Dr Anthony Leeds is Senior Lecturer in the Department of Nutrition & Dietetics at King's College London. He graduated in medicine from the Middlesex Hospital Medical School, London, UK in 1971. He conducts research on carbohydrate and dietary fibre in relation to heart disease, obesity and diabetes and continues part-time medical practice. He chairs the research ethics committee of King's College London, is a member of the Society of Authors, and in 1999 was elected a Fellow of the Institute of Biology.